imaginary **journe**

NEW LAMPS FROM OLD

24 fun ways to make new tales
from old plots

Rob Parkinson

Book 4 in the series 'Natural Storytellers'
Published by Imaginary Journeys
27 London Road, Tonbridge, Kent TN10 3AB UK
Tel/fax +44 (0) 1732 362356
E-mail: info@imaginaryjourneys.co.uk

www.imaginaryjourneys.co.uk

First published November 2007
© Rob Parkinson 2007

ISBN 13: 978-0-9549001-5-1

Imaginary Journeys catalogue no. IJ 204

NEW LAMPS FROM OLD

Contents

INTRODUCTION

The thief who is not caught becomes a king - saying

Human beings are notion thieves. We steal ideas and behaviours from each other all the time. It is one reason we're such a successful species, why we have developed cultures and indeed all sorts more, from fashions to sciences. Yet in story making in this particular culture, we're officially supposed to be original. It's not the done thing to appropriate other people's ideas – or at least, to admit it.

In fact we don't create stories from scratch. Each of us absorbs all sorts of patterns and templates for story making from everyday speech, from whatever oral traditions we are exposed to, from film and TV and newspapers and of course from books. Each of us imitates naturally as part of learning. You can see this very clearly in children's story making and telling, in which there are so often echoes of all sorts of things they have heard and read and seen. Indeed, the more they have heard and read and been encouraged to think about flexibly, the more likely they are to be able to make good new stories. The originality of human beings is in our ability to take an idea and not only run with it but chuck it around and bend it out of shape and re-clothe and disguise it in all sorts of improbable ways.

New Lamps from Old is the fourth in a series of booklets of oral games and other techniques for playing with and re-making stories. You could say that the theme of this one is stealing ideas and passing them off as your own, but that would miss something vital. The best stories and plot motifs have something about them that's better expressed in another metaphor, hinted at in the booklet's title with its slight mangling of the famous phrase in the tale of Aladdin. They are magic lamps you can use over and over again to make new ones, whilst still miraculously keeping the original.

The games in this set have been developed in hundreds of workshops over many years and across a broad age range, from approximately 7 years old to adults. Some 5 and 6 year olds also enjoy them, though unlike many games in other booklets, these all depend on some ability both to recall a plot and to see it as a flexible thing. Changing plots too much can confuse very young children.

Again, whilst many of these games appeal to children and have indeed been played and developed with many groups of children both in and out of the educational context, there's a lot adults can learn from them too. Anyone studying and practising storytelling as such will no doubt take whatever they need from them, but as with other games in the series there are many applications beyond what is usually thought of as 'the arts' – in fields such as therapy, counselling or emotional and moral education, where the concern is subtle change and development.

The book is divided into 3 sections. Part 1 features a series of games aimed at clearly establishing the notion of underlying frameworks and using them to make new tales. Part 2 features games that start from particular plots and motifs. These are presented in short, largely undeveloped form at the head of each game; they'll need elaborating if they are to come over as imaginatively engaging stories, by telling, by reading or listening to other versions of the same plot - and/or by playing the kinds of story stretching games in Book 3 *Yarn Spinning*. Some games depend on the particular plot or motif shown; others can be used with many other plots. I hope they'll suggest the many creative ways in which traditional plots can be used to develop imaginative story making and will lead to new experiments. The last 4 of these games (Nos 17 to 20) are, incidentally, more elaborate, so it's probably best to leave them until the others are familiar. Finally, Part 3 features a series of 4 solo games to develop important conscious skills of solo imagining.

As with other volumes, there are 3 kinds of note provided with the games.

General Note: This may include extra hints on ways to make the game effective as well as how to go on developing and adapting it. It's part of the spirit of playing these games (and of storytelling in general

I think) to treat rules as flexible and changeable, not set in stone, so please take the outline simply as a starting point.

Story Skills: Specific story telling and making skills practised in the game are signposted under this heading, sometimes with suggestions about how an oral game connects to the writing or telling of a story, sometimes with points about story skill development in general.

Interesting: As already mentioned, many game techniques can be focused differently for use in contexts such as counselling and therapy, health care, effective behaviour teaching or moral education etc Some of these uses are touched on here. This is an important field I've investigated thoroughly in recent years. Those who are interested in finding out more about this subject are referred to my book, *Transforming Tales*.

The theme of changing stories is hardly new. Some suggest that tradition is there for the taking, to be moulded, subverted and altered to suit the needs of the day. Traditionalists, on the other hand, can be found arguing that old stories should never be tinkered with, only passed on. I'd personally want to steer a course somewhere between these poles. Yes, stories can and should be changed to suit time, place and people – they always have of course, hence the many 'universal' plots and motifs that can be found wearing very different disguises in different cultures. But then again one should not slip into thinking there is no essence; one needs to learn to respect the depth and breadth of enduring and rich metaphor at the heart of many traditional patterns. Which one can learn to do precisely by playing with such patterns, stretching them out of and then back into shape in all sorts of ways, Which is what these games are about. This, incidentally, is where it all connects to the use of the story in real education – which I'd venture to say is education of the spirit, the essence that can be developed as more than a mimetic echo.

Rob Parkinson   November 2007

5.

PART 1.
FRAMES & TRANSPOSITIONS

Stories can be changed yet stay the same underneath. Not everyone knows this. But persuade anyone willing and able enough (young to old, amateur to professional) to make up an instant story and they'll commandeer all sorts of stray motifs and plots and re-clothe them to make their tale. The games in this first section introduce and practise the whole idea of the plot and its transposition to make new stories.

1. CHANGEABILITY

Changeability is a basic game for introducing and practising the transposition idea. As set out here, it's for adults and children over 7, though can be adapted for younger players. It's for 2 players or teams (**A & B**). The aim is to change a story in as many ways as possible whilst keeping the underlying pattern

First: A well known story is chosen and the story is divided into an equal number of approximate sections (Example: *Puss in Boots: 1. Miller dies & 3rd son gets cat. 2. Cat talks and gets boots 3. Cat visits the king 4. King and princess out in coach & find 3rd son stripped of clothes, introduced as The Marquis of Carabas.   4. Cat threatens workers in nearby fields and finds ogre's castle. 5. The cat tricks the ogre 6. King, Princess & 3rd son arrive at castle. Happy Ending.*

Then:

• **A** Changes the first part of the story in as many ways as possible - characters, place setting, age in which it happens and so on. (*It's not a mill in France, it's a sweet factory in Scotland. and there are 3 daughters, not sons. The third daughter gets the delivery truck.*)

• As these changes are explained, **B** asks questions to establish details of the stage (as in No.1 *Embroidery* in Book 3).*(What kind* *of sweets do they make? What kind of vehicle is the delivery truck?*)

• (Optional) When the game is familiar (or if there is a group leader to referee) **B** can also object if a) the story is not different enough or b) the plot has not been followed. **A** must adapt if the objection is justified.

• **B** changes the second part of the story, continuing the setting etc. already established. (*The delivery truck talks through an onboard computer. It gets luminous tyres that flash and change to every colour of the rainbow*). **A** asks the questions and/or raises objections.

• **A** changes the 3rd part... And so on through all the pairs of stages of the story

Finally (optional): The story is retold with all its changes. In group settings, pairs can go on to tell their new story to other pairs. Groups can simply go over the story together, smoothing over any small 'wrinkles' to make the new version work better.

General Note: It's useful to set out the number of ways in which the story can change. Time and place changes can be explored for example stories – ancient tales moving to modern or even futuristic settings, hot deserts becoming cold forests etc. Character changes range from simple (fox becomes dingo, rabbit becomes wallaby) to more complex (man becomes woman, animal becomes man etc). With the youngest children, the competitive elements of the game can be taken out and the transposition can be done as a simple collaboration. Developments of the game might restrict changes to one or two dimensions of change – characters stay the same but time and place changes; different characters and time; setting same or similar and so on.

Story skills: Understanding how stories change and stay the same should be a basic requirement of all story teaching and learning. When people learn a story, they learn not only the story but also the many variants of the story they and others can create from that story, the many elements they can take and adapt from that story.

Interesting: *Many life skills can be learned imaginatively from transposition exercises. Seeing that the same pattern can work in many different story scenarios is a training for seeing how the metaphorical patterns in stories can be applied to numerous different situations – and embedding the metaphorical pattern more firmly in the mind. (A simple example would be the* Good luck/bad luck *pattern in game 9 below). Also communicators need to be able to adapt a story to suit different audiences, clients, patients etc.*

2. PINK RINSE & THE 3 TIGERS

A competitive transposition game to follow on from *Changeability*. It is for two people or groups. The aim is to disguise a story that should be well known to the players (i.e. either a very well known children's story such as *Goldilocks & the 3 Bears* or a story with which all the players have been involved) so well that the other player/team don't guess what it is before the time limit or set number of questions is finished, following the guessing rules (see below).

First: Both groups/ players prepare a story, thinking of ways to change and disguise it as much as possible whilst retaining the underlying pattern. They agree on a time limit for the (later) guessing stage (usually 3 to 5 minutes) and/or on a limit to the number of questions (say 10).

Now:

• Players **A** tell their story. Players **B** guess what the original is. They are allowed 3 direct guesses and a number of indirect questions (i.e. not involving actual guesses as to what it is) about the story and there may be a time limit (see above).

• Players **B** tell their story and Players **A** guess according to the same rules.

- Each group or pair prepare another story and then play the game again. Or in a group workshop, change partners and try swapping the same stories, perhaps pausing first to improve the disguise.

General Note: *The idea of changing stories but keeping the pattern needs to be well established first, perhaps through a game like* Changeability. *Whilst adults and many teenagers and older children may seem to grasp the notion instantly, even so it's common to find people using only some elements of a plot, which is against the rules here.*

Story skills: *This game pushes the transposition idea further, asking players not only to use the plot in full but also to cover their tracks. Equally it encourages the guessing players to look out for the known plot – a skill that apparently gives Scooby-Doo and Columbo fans some difficulties. Learning to appreciate plotting and subtle variations on themes is an essential part of appreciating any literature. It's surprising that teachers often treat transposition exercises as peripheral curiosities.*

Interesting: *This game tests the ability to hold on to a pattern a little further and also to develop the skill of seeing through the disguise a plot is wearing – which, since we find ourselves involved in some repeating 'plots' too often in life, is a more useful everyday skill than might be obvious at first sight.*

3. FRAMING IT

- Young person sent to look after some important creatures for the community
- Young person is bored so sets off alarm for fun
- People duly alarmed – then cross
- Young person repeats trick – more annoyance
- There is a real danger but alarm ignored - people have learned that it means nothing

It doesn't take adults long to recognize Aesop's famous fable in this

5 point frame, though children who know the story can still take longer. It's fun to prepare several such frames and to see whether others can guess what the story is.

Formalized as a game, this works well for groups. The idea is to reduce as many stories as possible to an abstract frame of 5 (or perhaps 3 or 7) points or stages within a set time – say 10 minutes. The frame must outline the story well enough for others to guess what the original is, whilst not using any names and other details that will give it away too easily. (Just how abstract the frame can be expected to be will vary with age and experience of players - genderless terms like 'persons' and 'individuals' are less familiar to young players.)

A typical (and simple) way to play the game in a group would be:-

First (with those unfamiliar with the idea) thoroughly explore what is required with example frames such as the one above or perhaps made together and written on a board, flip chart pad etc.

Next everyone sets about making their series of frames based on any story the group can be assumed to know.

Finally group members take it in turns to present (i.e. read out or recite from memory – or display in writing or print) frames, which other group members must guess. Group members score a point for every frame guessed (but not judged as too obvious by the group leader/referee etc)

General: *With a little ingenuity, this can be further developed as a team game – though to give a motivation for guessing the original, members of the same team will do the guessing, scoring points for their team for each correctly guessed frame source. Frames made in this game can be used in other games.*

Story skills: *This teaches a lot about plot and rehearses that learning practically. A beginning-middle-end (hence apparently 3 point) structure is often taught to children for their story making. However, note that in many stories an elaborate introduction and an extended 'coda' can be (and often is) additional to the underlying plot structure. The number of points is arbitrary – though practically, many common story plots from tradition do fall into 3 to 7 stages, with 5 as the easiest mid point. Stories reduced to frames can be 'filled in' in new ways – as in the next game.*

Interesting: *Sometimes reducing a story in this way can help a person or group to see more clearly the vital and rewarding metaphorical structure in a story – as in the example frame in the next game and indeed in the Aesop's fable above. Making a relevant story into an abstract frame (and then perhaps re-clothing it as in Flesh on Bones below) can hence help the 'penny to drop' in counselling, coaching, tutoring etc.*

4. FLESH ON BONES

Here is a 5-stage story frame, something like those made in the previous game.

- Person living poor life believes he/she is unlucky
- Person is given a lucky charm (or similar) by someone believed to have magic powers
- Person's luck begins to change.
- Change in luck leads to major success in life and complete change of circumstance.
- After some time, the person finds that the charm really had no magical power at all.

There are many stories based roughly on this idea (I call the plot *The Talisman* - there's a version on my *Powerful Stories* double CD). It can be fleshed out in all sorts of very interesting ways.

An elaboration game similar to some in Book 3 *Yarn Spinning* such as No.1 *Embroidery* can be played with any story frame like this or with frames made in games such as No. 3 *Framing It* above. It works as a pair game or in a workshop group as described below.

First a storyteller (or pair or group of storytellers) is chosen and has to present the story frame one stage at a time.

Then the rest of the group ask him/her/them as many questions about each stage up to a set maximum number (5 or 7), designed to find out as much about the story so far and the characters involved as possible. (For example, in The Talisman frame, under point 1: *Who is this poor person? Why is he/she poor? What convinces this individual of his/her bad luck? Please describe this person's appearance. Please describe the place in which he/she lives?* Etc.)

Storytellers must answer as fully as possible, without copying any known story. (If the story they tell is too like a story known to the group, they are asked to change it.) Whatever they say is true for their version of the story – but must be kept consistent as they answer further questions. (A story set in space in the future can't suddenly move to New Zealand in 1832. If a character in the story is black-haired and strong, he or she can't suddenly be blond and weak etc). The group can challenge if the story falters and is inconsistent.

Finally (Optional) When all stages are complete, the storytellers re-tell the whole story with as many of the added details as possible.

General Note: As mentioned above, this is like other questioning games in the Natural Storytellers *series. The frame makes it more structured than open-ended creative games like* Fantastic Fibs *(Book 1* Tall Tale Telling *No 1) of course, whilst the set frame allows storytellers to be less fluent in narrative than* Embroidery, *so that it makes a good prelude to that game for some players.*

Story skills: Much that is interesting about a story and makes it live comes from the added detail. Yet being able to sort out what is essential to the plot gives one the power to add and embellish that plot in new ways. This is the theme explored in Book 3, Yarn Spinning *of course.*

Interesting: The way a person elaborates a plot can say much about them and their own concerns, sometimes including things they would not tell you in more formal communication. This is well worth listening to in 'change-focused' counselling etc situations. Sometimes also negotiating the way a story can be altered and developed differently can be loaded with personal meaning.

5. WHISPERINGS

When frames have been fleshed out into a story by individual players, in pairs or in smaller groups, it's good to play this passing it on/guessing game with a larger group. Players **A, B, C, D** (etc) can be individuals, pairs or small groups.

First players/groups/pairs etc. **A, B, C, D** etc. have made different stories from several possible frames (as in No 4, *Flesh on Bones* above). They do not know each other's frames and stories.

Then

- Players **A** tell a story on to players **B**, who tell their story in return. Meanwhile, players **C** and **D** (plus **E, F** etc, depending of group size) do the same thing with their different stories. In telling the story, the story and frame must not be revealed.

- All players next take the stories they have been told, play with them and alter them in as many ways as possible.

- Now **A** tells to **C** and **B** to **D** etc. Again groups play with and alter the latest stories they have been given. This goes on through a series of moves, with several stories circulating at the same time.

Finally: The resulting stories are told to the whole group who guess their 'lineage' (i.e. what the original frame and story was). Where there is doubt, stories can be traced back to reveal the original 'frame' by working through the different tellers

General note: The simple idea of altering and passing on stories without

knowing the original and then guessing what that original was can be used in various other ways to suit different numbers of players. The version given here assumes some fluency in making and telling tales. Compare this game with No 2 Pass it On in Book 1 Tall Tale Telling.

Story skills: *This game is, of course, modelling what goes on in both oral and literary traditions of story making, where plots and motifs mutate through many different forms. It's a good exercise in understanding how this works – as well as in creating tales from different models. It's also an exercise in developing a quick memory for stories, since players may be required to recall and play with several stories in the session.*

Interesting: *People of all ages inevitably latch on to different meanings for stories. It may well also be possible to bring out many complementary meanings in different stories. This game can be teaching players to be flexible in their understanding of narratives, which in turn feeds into more flexible thinking.*

6. FOOLING WITH FRAMES

- Agricultural mother and son team need to realise their chief asset...
- Son parts with asset for dubious future investment...
- Investment achieves extraordinary growth and boosts son to great heights
- Son involved in shenanigans with one of the big boys involving savings heist, gold standards and angelic music
- Connections are cut and the big boy's fall leaves the team happy

This is a very well known children's story reduced to an outline frame but wearing the kind of tongue-in-cheek disguise adults might give it whilst playing this guessing game. It might not make much sense to many children, but they can still play the game at their own level once

14.

familiar with the transposition idea. (*1. Boy's mum sends him out to sell an important creature. 2. Boy gets no money and seems to make a bad deal. 3. Something grows high and leads to a climb etc*)

Again it involves generally well-known stories or other tales particularly familiar to the group. Again it's for 2 players or teams. The aim is for one side to present a disguised story frame and for the opposing side to guess what the story is as soon as possible. The scoring system described below can be adjusted as appropriate and, may be best left out when first trying the game with younger players.

First both players/teams choose stories to be summarised in a suitably disguised 5- (or 3- or 7-) point frame. To avoid the possibility that they will choose the same story, a series of suitable story titles can be written on slips of paper, which are then folded and put into a hat or bag to be selected. Or the 2 players/teams can take 2 different lists of possible stories.

(*Advisable at least when the game is new.*) Players can spend a set period of time (say 5 minutes) thinking about/discussing their frames and improving the disguise. The finalized frame can be written down.

Now

- Players **A** read out or recite the first point in their frame. Players **B** can guess at this stage. If they get it right, they get 5 points but if they are wrong then one point goes to **A**.

- If the story was not guessed from the first point, the second point in the frame is presented. Again **B** can guess, this time being able to score 4 points for a correct guess but with the same penalty of 1 point to **A** if wrong.

- As long as the story has not been guessed, **A** continues to present the summary, point by point. If it's guessed at 3, **B** scores 3, if at 4 **B** scores 2, if at 5 **B** scores 1 (whilst **A** scores 1 point for incorrect guesses at each stage). If it's not guessed at all, **A** also scores an extra point.

- (Optional) If the story is guessed earlier than the 5th stage, any remaining stages can be presented to check that they 'match'. In a group, a referee (usually the group leader) can judge whether these stages match the original properly.

- Once Players **A** have presented their story frame, Players **B** present theirs and again points are scored. Several rounds can be played with different stories. The overall winner is the player/team with most points.

General note: *This game builds on skills built up in previous games, so younger players will need to work through those games. Though it's similar to No 3. Framing It and follows on well from it, note that the aim is reversed. Children as young as 7 have been able to play this very happily with enough preparation, whilst considerably younger children enjoy guessing suitably disguised story frames. As implied, the degree of disguise players will understand and use depends on age and experience.*

Story skills: *Quite a sophisticated understanding both of story and the kinds of words that can be used to describe it is developed here. Being able to outline a story in this playful way demands advanced conceptualization based on a knowledge of more than a few stories and the kinds of things that happen in them.*

Interesting: *It is sometimes revealing to note the different sides of a story that emerge through different framings of it – what is seen to be essential by different people. Story frames in general have some important therapeutic uses as outlined in my book,* Transforming Tales. *For example, when the frame demands a positive outcome (castle freed from enchantment; group or individual repel an alien invasion etc.) filling out the frame into a story can be 'solution focused', becoming a metaphorical rehearsal of personal change and development.*

PART 2. GAMES WITH PLOTS

Very many old plots and motifs crop up in different countries with quite different cultures, wearing quite different clothes, yet remain the same underneath. Some go on being recycled to this day – elements of quite ancient tales can be hidden inside modern fictions and films. All of the 14 games in this section start from a traditional plot or motif, usually set out in brief summary form first. The summaries are not supposed to be the only introduction to the tale. They might be told by a workshop leader in a group situation, read in a book, listened to in another version on CD if possible or explored and developed into longer stories first through games in Book 3 *Yarn Spinning*. Some games depend on the particular plot or motif illustrated; some (like the first game below) can work with many other tales. They can all provide examples of how to play creatively with a story.

7. GENIES IN BOTTLES

Khalifah the fisherman casts his nets each day on the furthest shores of Arabia, praying for the luck that will feed his wife and thirteen children. One day he finds a bottle in his nets, barnacle-encrusted but clearly marked with the Seal of Solomon. When he opens it, out comes a huge genie. Instead of offering him wishes and fortune, however, this genie vows to kill him by way of revenge on humankind for centuries spent under the sea. Khalifah, thinking quickly, asks the genie how it could possibly fit into a bottle. The genie, put on its mettle, demonstrates by shrinking and jumping back in. Khalifa corks it up again. Now he has the genie in the bottle. It begs to be let out again and promises wishes and wealth. What should Khalifa do next?

The well known Arabian Nights tale is presented as a dilemma story here – a story that ends in a question like this one. This kind of tale is a great way to start an imaginative discussion. The following group game extends the dilemma story (and sharpens any possible discussion) by making it into a story telling/transposing game. It needs at least 2 (and up to 5) tellers. It will work as well with many other short dilemma tales.

First a pair or group of storytellers is chosen to tell a version of *The Genie in the Bottle* (or other dilemma tale)

Then

- Storytellers tell the tale.They must not tell the received version, but a new one. *(It won't be a genie in a bottle, but it could be a witch in a bag or a ghost in a box. It won't be a fisherman, but it could be a florist or a carpenter.)*

- Listeners raise questions. These should be about how the new version works by comparison with the old one. (*Why did you choose a florist and how is she like that fisherman? How is she different?* etc.) Storytellers take it in turns, answering single queries.

- At the dilemma point, the 2 (or more) storytellers tell different versions of what happens next. (*Getting rid of the bottle ? Making a bargain with the genie? Letting it out?* etc.)

- Listeners can now be asked to vote on their preferred direction or they can simply discuss the different options and offer any other ones.

Whatever storytellers say in answer to any questions at any stage in the story is accepted, providing it is consistent with the story so far.

General note: *The genie in the bottle plot has moved through many different cultural settings and oral traditions – the devil caught in a box or a bag, the fairy in a pot, the troll under a stone and so on. Dilemma stories exist in many traditions; modern ones surface on the internet from time to time. They seem to have been particularly popular in West African oral tradition (see for example No 15 The 3 Wizards & the Forest).*

Story skills: *Narrative dilemmas are not confined to formal dilemma tales of course – exploring the dilemma characters face in any story is a useful part of story teaching. A good metaphor for a story is the road, which of course has many sidetracks, crossroads, detours etc. The 'dilemma point' procedures in this game can be extended to some of those other crossroads etc – what possible different directions are there here and there and there?*

Interesting: *Dilemma stories are a traditional way of teaching people to think and imagine things through, taking a broader view. Unlike the habit of sealing off meaningful fables from further ruminations with a trite moral, the dilemma tale asks people to consider carefully how the story should go on – and why it should do so. This game forces players to consider the dilemma even more. The genie-in-the-bottle metaphor in the example story, incidentally, can be powerful in use with people experiencing unpredictable mental states.*

8. WISHES THREE

A king has a marvellous beard. Everyone praises it – the way to this king's favour is through doing just that. The king, however, wants to be sure that it is the finest in the world. So when a wizard gives him a magic mirror that gives three wishes, he promptly wishes that the royal beard should be the finest ever in all the world. At once the beard grows until it fills his whole castle, but now he is trapped inside his own beard. Desperately and without thinking, he wishes he'd never ever grown a beard – and is suddenly confronted with his own naked face and pink, chubby cheeks. Again he's unhappy - he's sure people will laugh at him. The only thing is to use the third wish to get back his beard just as it was before the wishing began.

This is a brief summary of the story told on my first story CD, *Will's Clogs* (Imaginary Journeys IJ102). Several more 3 wishes tales are available in a free download available from the downloads section of the Imaginary Journeys website. The *Wishes 3* game can be played by 2

people or in both small and large groups. The storyteller gets three wishes and aims to get and keep what he or she wants. The partner or group aim to stop this happening within the rules.

First The storyteller is chosen and has to say where and how he or she gets the 3 wishes – from a lamp or a ring or a computer etc. Questioning games from other booklets such as *Fantastic Fibs* (No 1, Book 1) or *Embroidery* (No 1 Book 3) can be used to make this 'fib' more real and developed.

Then

- Storytellers say what their first wish will be. (It is against the rules of the game to cheat by asking for endless wishes.)

- The partner or group now spoil this wish. They are not allowed to say that the wish doesn't work but must find a way in which it works in an unexpected and difficult way – as in *The King's Beard,* summarised above.

- Storytellers must respond to this, getting themselves out of the mess and on track again. The simplest thing is to wish the result of the first wish away (as the king does), though that will mean using the second wish and could be a disaster. Perhaps it's possible to use the second wish cleverly to make the first wish come true as well as getting something else. Perhaps it's possible to dodge the results of Wish 1 without using Wish 2 yet.

- Wish 2 is used (if not used already). Again the other player(s) try to spoil this wish by making it work in a way the wisher didn't expect

- The storyteller has to respond to this consequence. Again the simple route is to wish that everything is just as it was before the wishing began – though there will now be no more wishes. Again, there may be cleverer ways to save the advantages gained and find more without using the last wish.

- Wish 3 is used if not used already. If it has already been used to go back to safety (just as things were before the wishes), then the game ends here. If not, Wish 3 can be followed by more spoiling involving unexpected interpretations and consequences of the wish, though the storyteller can again respond by turning those consequences to the good.

Finally: The stages of the game make a new 3 wishes story, with the storyteller as the hero or heroine. This can be re-told

General note: *In workshops etc, it's useful to try the game a couple of times with the group before sending group members away to work in pairs. In this situation, several 'spoils' can be suggested for each wish, before one (only) is chosen. The rule about not wishing for more wishes has to be stressed – but clever ways around it might be allowed.*

Story skills: *The 3 wishes plot has many variants. It's a good plot to experiment with – it's not difficult to invent dozens of examples of 3 wishes tales, exploring why different characters in different settings might make the same kinds of mistake in predicting the consequences of wishes.*

Interesting: *'Be careful of what you want – you may well get it.' Anyone who has lived more than a very sheltered existence will appreciate the truth of this maxim – and its connection with 3 wishes plots. But more interesting than spelling out morals (learn this because it's good for you!) is how this game can provide direct imaginative rehearsal of what can happen when you do actually get what you want.*

9. GOOD LUCK/BAD LUCK

At the end of the year, a boy is talking about school. 'The teacher we had this year was really strict and she never smiled. If you made the smallest mistake in your stories, you had to re-write them.' 'That was bad luck,' insists his friend from another school. 'Oh I don't know about that,' the boy says. 'She made us do really good stories and then she put them into this big competition and we won a prize.' 'Good luck,' says his friend, but again the boy is doubtful. 'The prize turned out to be a balloon ride. But when we were up in the sky, it was suddenly very windy and wet. The balloon got blown into a big tree and they couldn't get it out.' 'That was bad luck then,' 'Oh no, we all climbed down the tree and went off to play.' 'Good luck?' 'Maybe, but without our weight, the balloon blew away and the wind carried it all the way to America.' 'Wow, that's incredible! Bad luck for the balloon owners though.' 'Yes, but not for us. Our teacher was still in it!'

The good luck, bad luck game is based on the pattern in the many (not always jokey) stories like this one. It is for 2 players or teams. It works like this:

First decide on a rough scenario for the story – time and place setting, central character or characters, real world or magical etc. Set a time limit for the main game (say 5 minutes)

Then

> • **A** describes what seems to be good luck for the central character(s) Three things/circumstances etc. should be described to give a picture of this.

> • **B** describes how this leads into or gives way to (or has all the time been) bad luck, again using up to 3 events, things, facts etc..

> • **A** now turns this into good luck (again using up to 3 points)

> • **B** turns it into bad luck...

> .... And so on, through as many different 'rounds' of good luck/bad as possible within the time limit. At the end of this time, the player speaking can conclude the 'story' with what seems to be either good luck or bad.

Finally (optional) Go over the story that emerged and note the details. Count the 'rounds' of good and bad luck managed and (in a group) perhaps compare these with other pairs of players. Re-tell the story as a story to someone else or to the group. Perhaps add an ending tag about never knowing what is good or bad luck.

General note: Again it's easier for players (especially younger ones) to pick up the game if a version of the story is first told. It's worth pointing out (if possible using an extra example) that good luck/bad luck stories don't have to end with a joke-like punch line and could even be serious in tone. Counting the rounds of good luck/bad can be made competitive in group situations.

Story skills: Good luck/bad is an example of what seems the simplest kind of plot and yet many popular soap operas work on this principle, whilst the working out of intertwined fates and the revelation that bad luck is good and vice versa has been the subject of classic novels. This game again leaves players with a story that can be refined through re-telling and writing. The effectiveness of 3 point descriptions is explored in Book 3, Yarn Spinning.

Interesting: Good luck/bad stories (perhaps in guises such as the well known Chinese one presented on my Powerful Stories *double CD) are very useful for therapists, counsellors and others working with clients who tend to see things in limited terms of personal bad luck. The game can involve such people more directly in the re-framing effort involved in noticing that the bottle may be half full, not half empty and can even be described in other ways: especially if they're obliged to take the good luck side.*

10. THE MAGIC CHASE

Jack works for the wizard on a promise that he'll learn the magic, but gets no instruction at all, only chores. Eventually he steals a peep at the magic book and learns the magic of transformation. He also understands that the wizard will kill him when he finds out, so he turns himself into a fish and swims away along a nearby stream. The wizard spots him and turns into an otter to catch the fish. Jack becomes a dove flying high and away but the wizard becomes an eagle to swoop on the dove. Jack sees the flash of a ring on the finger of a princess outside a castle below and becomes the stone on the ring. The wizard glides *down and becomes a minstrel of such inspired skill that the king asks him to choose his reward. The disguised wizard chooses the ring, but when the princess stretches out her hand to deliver the ring, it jumps off her hand into the castle fire. The wizard becomes tongs to pull out the ring, but the ring jumps out onto the flagstones and becomes a grain of corn. The wizard becomes a cockerel to gobble up the grain, but Jack becomes a fox to kill that cockerel. Then he changes himself to a handsome young man in fine clothes. He and the princess fall in love and are married the next day. If they're not dead yet they are living in that castle to this day.*

This is a brief summary of a tale that can take around 20 minutes to tell with elaboration. The motif of the transformation chase/contest comes into a lot of traditional stories from many different countries. Sometimes the 'thief' escapes, sometimes he or she is caught by the wizard figure. The transformation game is a good way to start using this plot and demands some quick thinking. It's for 2 players (or teams). One player takes the Jack role and tries to escape; the other is in the wizard role and tries to catch Jack.

First

- Decide on who is Jack and who is the wizard. (Or decide to be different figures – Mary and the witch, Zog and the Alien etc.)

- Also (optional) decide how the magic is obtained – is it from a book of spells or an internet site involving scientific formulae?

- Is the game set in the ancient past, the distant future or the present? (If played according to stricter rules, this will affect what it is possible to change into – cavemen might not know much about rockets for example.)

- Is danger involved before the getting of the 'magic'?

- Will it be described as magic or is there some way to alter this?

Now: The Chase *(We'll use Jack and the Wizard for convenience.)*

- Jack describes his first change to escape the wizard *(I change into a... and get away by...)*.
- The wizard decribes his first change to catch Jack (*But I change into a ...to catch you by....)*.
- Jack makes another change to escape the wizard.
- The wizard changes again to catch Jack....
- ...and so on through as many changes as it takes for Jack to beat the wizard or the wizard to catch Jack.

Finally: Re-tell the transformations in the game and make a note of them. Invent a 3-part story involving all of the changes (middle) plus the preliminary section (beginning) explaining how the Jack figure got involved with the wizard figure and read the spell book (or whatever) and bringing the story to a more complete conclusion (end).

General note: *Young players who have been told an elaborated version of the chase story can often play the chase game together with very little explanation, though also often forget some of their transformations when asked to re-tell. However the other stages can be added later, as the game is played again, perhaps with encouragement to spend longer imagining each change. The story can be told to others or written down. Repeated playing can encourage competition over the number of pairs of changes (1.fish/otter, 2.dove/eagle etc.) achieved by pairs of players.*

Story skills: *This is a good game for warming up 'imagination muscles'. With repeated use and development of all stages, it also trains the ability to think imaginatively, to anticipate consequences, to remember and to adapt rapidly. And of course the game, when played 'all through', should leave players with new magical transformation stories.*

Interesting: *Stay cool inside and you'll come through, the quarry can be victor in the end. – these might seem to be some of the possible morals here. But again, the game gives an imaginative rehearsal whose practical harvest can be improved emotional attitudes and abilities: this or that might be scary, but if I use the magic of transformation, I can make myself stronger/quicker/ cleverer/ bolder etc.*

11. STRONGER THAN

A forester goes into the forest to chop wood. As he marches along, he thinks how strong he is – with his great axe, he could fell any of these great trees all around him. He feels stronger and more alive than anything. As he thinks this, he is passing a rocky cliff in the woods. A rock has been dislodged from the cliff and fetches him a glancing blow, knocking him to the ground. He picks himself up, rubbing his head in stunned amazement at this immediate answer to his thought and he says.' I see. I understand. I may be strong, but the rock is stronger.' Then there is even more amazement, because he hears a voice that must come from the rock itself. 'Yes, I am strong, but not as strong as the rain that washes the rock and soaks the cliff. It was the rain that swelled the crack and made me fall.'

The forester turns to the rain and says that it must then be the strongest of all things. Today the rain can speak too. It tells him that it is not as strong as the wind that blows it wherever it chooses. He turns to the wind, but the wind says that it is not as strong as the mountain, which it cannot shift at all. He goes to the mountain, but the mountain explains that it is not a strong as the bird that taps its beak each day on its peak and wears it away, bit by bit. He finds the bird, but the bird says it is not as strong as the arrow that could pierce it. He finds the arrow, but the arrow says it is not as strong as the bow that fires it. He finds the bow but it says that it is not as strong as the arm that bends it. And the arm is his own arm. So he learns that he is weak and strong and that all things work together.

This pattern has variants from many parts of the world, from Africa to Japan and beyond. The story and the game based on it both have something in common with *The Magic Chase*. Again it's for 2 players or teams (**A** & **B**) The aim is to invent a story around a chain of things, each apparently stronger than the last, but eventually reaching something that is stronger than the last thing but weaker/dependent on the central character(s), showing that things are interdependent. (God or any other absolute, all-powerful being is not allowed into the game, which must focus on worldly powers and things.) The person who can 'loop the chain' in this way wins the game, though this can't be done until at least 4 'stronger thans' have been brought in – a number that can be varied, as explained below.

First

Choose a central character or characters and an opening scenario. Decide on how many 'stronger than' moves must be played before you try to loop back to the beginning.

`Now

- **A** describes the first thing that is stronger than the central character(s) and how this is discovered

- B describes something that is stronger than this and how this is discovered .

- **A** describes something stronger and how the character meets and interacts with it.

- **B** does likewise.

- ... And so on, except that players who have agreed on a 4 move game may now try to loop back to the beginning, whilst in a 5 move version this would happen in the next round (etc).

- (Optional) Setting a time limit for the whole game is a useful way to stop endless chains that are impossible to remember.

Finally go back over the series of 'stronger than' things. These will give the bones of a new 'stronger than' story.

General note: In group situations, there can be an element of competition between pairs playing the game to see who can make the longest chain before looping to the ending. An open-ended game where you look for as many 'stronger thans' as possible with no 'looping' can even be made to work with 4 and 5 year old children when adult led – and of course the adult can always add a loop anyway. Older players can go on to develop games based on different concepts – Cleverer than, Faster Than, More beautiful Than etc.

Story skills: Chain stories like this one illustrate how an effective story can be built up from very simple elements and perceptions. Older players can go on to develop told and written chain stories that hide the folk model more completely behind more 'streetwise' surface description. These kinds of stories also lend themselves to adaptation as rhythmic verse and song lyrics.

Interesting: The wise teaching in the original folk tale subtly questions the kind of egoism endemic in our own society and world view, stressing interdependence. The game can underline this again because of the direct imaginative involvement in creating a new version. Perfectionism, utopianism and matters of low or high self esteem are personal and group themes both counsellors and educationalists may find themselves addressing. Played as 'Better than', 'More perfect than' or 'Cooler than' or even 'More miserable than', this game is a very good teaching/therapeutic tool.

12. THE TAILOR'S COAT

A tailor had to make his way in a new land. His only treasures were his own superb skills, a little money and a bolt of wonderful, very rare rainbow-coloured cloth. With this, he set to work and made an unusual and very stylishly cut coat which he wore everywhere. Soon he had customers who wanted similar coats in cloth they brought him. He hired premises and worked hard and prospered.

Things were going well, but then the coat was spattered by a passing carriage and the whole look of it was spoiled. Wasting no time, he set to work and made a splendid, dramatic looking cloak from the undamaged parts– the original bolt of cloth had all been used up. He wore this too. People loved it and again wanted their own versions. His

28.

business grew and he'd months of orders for cloaks.

Another accident ruined parts of the cloak, but there was enough left to make a waistcoat. When that began to wear, he turned the best bits into a hat. When that fell into a fire, he pulled it out and used the unscorched bits to make a scarf – then a tie, then a kerchief. Lastly he made, from last fragments of the wonderful cloth that had been all those things, 3 special buttons, which he wore on his court robes (by now he was the royal tailor). When the last of the buttons wore out, he had enough left for a story to last the rest of his life. This is the story and it's still not worn out.

A story that's almost standard repertoire amongst modern storytellers, the simple pattern in it is quite easy to transpose into all sorts of settings. Hence you get *The Carpenter's Chest, The Widow's Jumper* or *The God's Gift* for example. The aim of this game is to make more such variants, with roughly the same circular ending point. It's a verbal tennis game once more for 2 players or teams **A** & **B** , who alternate in developing the new pattern modelled on the old one:-

First get to know the original pattern thoroughly.

Then follow this sequence

- **A**1. Choose the craft or art: not a tailor but a...*(carpenter? embroiderer? painter?)*
- **B**1. Not a wonderful bolt of cloth but... (r*are timber? gold thread? fine canvas?*)
- **A**2 The first creation using this marvellous material was.....
- **B**2 Though this was good, after a time x happened to spoil it....
- **A**3 So from what was left, y was now made
- **B**3 Though this worked well, after a time something else happened to spoil it
- **A**4 So from what was left z was made...
- And so on, with **B** suggesting what spoils or wears or changes each creation and **A** making new things from what is left until **A** &

B agree - nothing was left but a story

Finally go back over the story that emerged and work out details before telling the story to someone else.

General note: *A story with a simple chain like this one is quite easy to learn and to improvise around. It makes a rewarding starting point for novice storytellers —it doesn't matter exactly what items the tailor (or whatever) makes as long as they are possible for a tailor, so there's immediate scope for playful changes. In group workshops, comparing different versions of the pattern that come through the game can be more than interesting.*

Story skills: *As different skill sets and materials are used with the pattern, skills of description are being stretched in many directions. Sometimes a telling won't be convincing until tellers find out more about the way the skill works or about the nature of the material. Research is another facet of good story making and telling.*

Interesting: *This plot can sometimes gain in depth through transposing it to different settings and skill sets, particularly when the material that is used and re-used is made more marvellous and unique. If it's ordinary cloth/timber/ thread, the tale seems to be only about economizing and being thrifty. If the 'cloth' always has some new facet that can be revealed through new workings, the central metaphor could become more complex and useful.*

13. THE NOISY HOUSE

A man lives all alone, apart from his dog. He thinks the house where he lives much too noisy. He goes to a woman in the village he reckons is a witch and asks for a spell to make it quiet. The witch lends him her black cat and he takes it home, but his dog chases the cat. The barks and mews and screeches echo round the house. He goes back to the witch, who now insists he take her goat and put it in the house. The goat bleats and butts the dog, which hence howls as well as barking whilst the cat screeches. Again, he goes back to the witch but now it's her six grandchildren who must accompany him home, where they are soon leaping around, screaming and shouting and chasing he dog and the cat and the goat. There is pandemonium. Suddenly the old woman arrives, raises her hand and the children stop, the goat stops, the dog stops and so does the black cat. 'Spell done!' she says. And she marches off with her cat and goat and children. After that the surprised man goes back into the house and suddenly realizes that it's really the most peaceful place on earth.

This folk-tale plot recurs in many other forms. It's easy to make new versions by changing 'noisy' and 'house' to comparable things. To play a solo or collaborative group transposition game based on the pattern once it has been taken in and learned:

First make four sets of words printed on separate small pieces of paper, card etc:

- The first comes from 'noisy' and includes sound (noise), sight, smell, taste, feeling (body), feeling (emotional) and perhaps size, shape (and any others).
- The second set is generated from 'house' is made up of words that are possible alternatives to house – castle, tent, town, country, place, coat, shoes, pot etc.
- The third set is comprised of alternatives to 'man' – from girls and boys to mythical monsters.
- The fourth is based around alternatives to witch – genie, sprite, wizard, alchemist etc.

Now the 2 different sets of slips are placed in different containers (bags, hats etc.) and you draw one slip or card from each set. Your cards might say 'sight' 'town' and 'dragon'. Your story will perhaps be about a dragon that finds the look of a town (say) too bright and sharp looking so he finds a genie and....

This can also be a fun group story making game. Everyone can contribute suggestions for the new tale, decide how it works then tell it to another group. Or it can be played competitively, with players or groups drawing the ingredients of their tale from the 3 pools and preparing versions based on them for a contest of tales.

General note: *Like* The Tailor's Coat, The Noisy House *is an excellent pattern for new storytellers to learn and vary playfully. The 'chain' is quite easy to recall and tinkering with the pattern can happen naturally.The game, however, can stretch ideas about how the tale can be altered beyond what comes up naturally.*

Story skills: *Originality is sometimes thought of as more the province of the writer or poet than that of the storyteller. Nothing could be further from the truth. Storytelling can be a highly creative craft; as illustrated here, a short pattern can be varied endlessly. Exercises like this one should be a vital part of a real storyteller's training.*

Interesting: The Noisy House *provides another very useful, very flexible metaphor for anyone working directly for pyschological change. It can say very relevant things to a person dealing with chronic pain, concentration or anger difficulties and many other concerns. Again involvement in remaking the tale through the game and using imagery and settings relevant to the person can make it more powerful.*

14. THE MIDAS CHALLENGE

The tale of King Midas and his golden touch, from Greek mythology, is so well known that people even talk of having 'the Midas touch', when they mean that a person has the knack of making any project they are involved in go well. This is not, of course, quite what happened with Midas, who wished that everything he touched would literally turn to gold and soon found how cold and unwelcoming a world made all from gold could be – and indeed soon wished to lose his golden touch.

This group or pair game follows on well from the previous game, sharing some procedures. It also has something in common with both No 9 *Good Luck/Bad Luck* and No 7. *Wishes Three*.

First get to know a version of *King Midas and the Golden Touch* through reading and listening and/or telling. Play some elaboration games from Book 3 *Yarn Spinning* with the pattern and imagine it through using *Imaginer* games from Part 3.

Now make some lists, rather like those in *The Noisy House*.
> • The first will be a series of alternatives for things/ situations/ people etc. to transform things into instead of gold, from jewels or chocolate to (say) 'green growing things' or 'worshipping fans'.
> • The second will be substitutes for touch – breath, speaking, singing, tasting, glance etc..
> • The third can be alternatives to king (or queen) - celebrity, general, teacher, president etc. (Genderless terms can be easiest in mixed groups.)

Next choose a King or Queen Midas equivalent.

> • 'Midas' draws words from the separate pools and will aim to make the best of this. His/her first task is to say a little about the character he/she has taken on in this game, why he/she wants this gift and what wonderful things will be done with it as soon as the magic works.

> • The other player(s) or group now come up with a drawback. The Midas character has to explain how he/she will solve this problem and do more wonderful things. Magic is not allowed now – it has to be a practical solution that makes the gift (say) more controllable (*e.g. in the original, Midas might start wearing gloves*). The only magic allowed at any stage is wishing the gift away again, but that will be accepting defeat at that stage.

> • As soon as the solution is described, the other player(s) can either challenge the solution (*e.g. the gloves will turn to gold)* or present a new difficulty (not both). Again Midas must solve the

problem (*a goldsmith provides special gold-handling material* for the gloves) or wish the gift away.

• And so on through an agreed number of moves (say up to 5). If the Midas character runs the gauntlet of the five tests, he/she wins the Midas Challenge. (The number of tests can be increased as the game is repeated.)

Finally: Again each round of the game makes a new story, based on the Midas legend – though sometimes 'Midas' will keep the golden touch equivalent.

General Note: Alternatives to 'golden' can stay simple for younger players. Older players can get more complicated and the alternatives can be written down at greater length. An extra 'pool' specifying genre and setting can be added, again for older and more experienced players.

Story Skills: Familiar mythology is often a rich source of ideas for new stories as many writers have found. In this case, taking a broad view of 'golden' and 'touch' can be an exercise in liberating some of that potential, from which one can progress to further transpositions of mythical themes..

Interesting: The Midas legend has its moral teaching of course and playing the game can enhance a perception of this, particularly since it demands a wide application and re-interpretation of the same metaphor. But equally the demand that the Midas challenge be taken on – that it's always possible to work with and minimize what seems to have become a disability – is useful and life-enhancing.

15. THE THREE WIZARDS & THE FOREST

In Africa once there were three wizards on a journey. They came to a great forest. It was dense and thick and a person might spend days lost in it. There were dangerous beasts and poisonous snakes lurking in the shadows. All three wizards knew that they did not wish to enter that forest, so they each used their magic powers in their own way. (These were powers they could use only to benefit themselves.)

The first took a small piece of string and, using a word of power, made it into a rope, lassoed a passing cloud and hauled himself up onto it. He allowed the breeze to blow him over the forest to the other side where he climbed down the rope, turned it back into string and went on his way.

The second took out a magic box, opened it up and, using another word of power, commanded the forest and all that was in it to enter. He closed the box, walked across the empty space where the forest had been and, when he got to the other side, opened the box again and ordered the forest and all back, exactly as everything had been before. He also travelled on.

The third took a small pipe, and blew through it the shape and the sound of yet another word of power. At once a mighty whirlwind arose and hurled forest and creatures to scatter in fragments a thousand miles away. Then he walked across the empty wastes and went on his way, leaving behind a desert that is there to this day.

Which of those three wizards was the greatest?

This is based on a dilemma pattern common in West African oral tradition. The pair or team game based on it will yield further episodes in the adventures of the three wizards or similarly powerful beings.

First get to know the pattern of this story and imagine it thoroughly, perhaps using the *Imaginer* from the final section of this booklet. Discuss/think through how differently the powers of each wizard work and what kinds of other things they might typically do. Also discuss the question at the end.

Now

- **A** says whether the tale is to be about the wizards or will change to witches or demons or mad scientists or aliens or any equivalent that can be made to work.
- **B** says what the challenge is (*cross a sea filled with sharks/ a desert/ a pit of fire etc*).
- **A** describes how the first wizard (or whatever) meets the challenge. This should somehow resemble the way of the first wizard, who left the forest untouched. **B** should question the solution if it is out of character (for example were this 'wizard' to move or destroy a mountain) and **A** can be asked to adjust or alter it.
- **B** now describes how the second wizard (etc) uses magic (or whatever) to deal with the challenge in a manner that is like the way of the second wizard (i.e. can involve total power over the challenge but will end by leaving things as they were at the outset). **A** can challenge if the match is not good (for example, if the wizard doesn't have enough power or leaves things very different) and **B** must adjust or alter.
- **A** and **B** both propose and discuss ways that the third wizard totally destroys the challenge.
- .(Optional) **A** and **B** propose and discuss an answer to the question of which is the greatest.

Finally: tell the new story, either ending with the question or giving an answer to it.

General Note: There is usually no shortage of ideas for re-workings of this plot, some highly inventive. A 10 year old boy suggested as an alternative for the 2nd wizard traversing the forest a clock that wound time backwards, so that the trees would be only shoots and the creatures eggs and cubs, then winding it forwards again. A series of tales about 3 wizards (or whatever) makes a good group presentation.

Story skills: This game demands that the way of each wizard stay consistent with the tendency shown in the original. This is a good exercise in being consistent with characters as well as in metaphor.

Interesting: *The simplicity of this tale belies the powerful metaphor it contains, which sums up some influential ways of solving problems on both global and personal levels. Involving a person inclined to look for solutions on the zap! pow! model of Wizard 3 in seeing the 'bleak desert' of consequences through the tale and game can be powerfully affective for example.*

16. SLIDING DOWN MOONBEAMS

A naive young man decided to break into a rich man's house to steal some money. One moonlit night, he climbed up onto the roof, ready to creep in through a window once the rich man and his wife were asleep. The rich man, however, spotted him, guessed what he was at and began a loud conversation with his wife. With many sly winks and nods to her, he loudly confessed that he had made all his money as a thief himself. She need not worry however: he had never and would never be caught because he had discovered a marvellous secret for making a quick escape. This was no more and no less than the ability to leap onto any bright moonbeam and slide down it to make a quick getaway. These moonbeams would be, he insisted, just like these now shining through the window. If only people knew... At this the young man, seized with enthusiasm for the idea, jumped wildly onto what he took to be a moonbeam and...

What should happen next in this old tale? There are two quite different directions for stories like this. The first is the obvious one – and indeed is what happens in the version from the medieval *Gesta Romanorum*, which provided the model for this summary: the young man falls to ground and is soon caught by the forces of law. But elsewhere, the equivalent of, the leap onto the moonbeam is a moment of pure magic: the young man's passionate belief and hidden good nature makes him able to defy gravity and actually slide down a moonbeam. Or some natural fluke works in his favour at this point – a whirlwind or a passing hay wagon.

This game starts from these divergent possibilities. It is for 2 players or teams, **A** & **B** with a third group of listeners (**C**). It takes the dilemma principle illustrated in the last game and in *Genies in Bottles* (No 7) further and the procedure can be used with any tale with this kind of alternative outcome.

First get to know the basic pattern of the story very well.

   • Players **A** work out a version of the story in which the thief will meet justice when he rashly tries to slide down the moonbeam. To get listeners (**C**) to sympathize with their versions, they might paint the thief as a villain as well as a fool, someone who deserves to be tricked. Their take on the rich man could be that he is honest and quick witted. They will want listeners (**C**) to laugh at how he tricks the thief.

   * Players **B** meanwhile create a version of the tale where (perhaps) the deserving if gullible young man has some justification for robbing the rich man, who is mean and arrogant and always thinks he can get the better of anyone. Hence the miracle or quirk of fate will be welcome and could perhaps lead to the rich man himself being tricked or some other form of justice.

Finally: The 2 stories are presented to the audience **C**, who may then simply vote on which story works best. Or, for more sophisticated groups, they (or a leader) may award points out of 10 for qualities such as characterization, believability, scene setting and so on.

General note: At first sight, this game seems to demand rather developed storytelling skill. My experience is that many players who have not done much formal tale telling quickly grasp the idea of how the same story can be shaped in different ways given different biases. Many 9, 10 and 11 year old players have been as stimulated as adult groups by the idea into some tremendous character exaggerations and sub plots.

Story skills: *Here the story is changed as the motivations of the characters are adjusted and explored to make different endings work. A vital part of learning about stories is seeing how the same plots and motifs can be shaped quite differently- and indeed how character and plot may be intertwined in the process. Note that the audience can be learning a lot and applying it in making their judgements.*

Interesting: *Re-shaping a story to make a different, optimistic ending can be an empowering exercise. A depressed, temporarily wheel-chair bound client was once affected very positively in a therapeutic setting by skilful play with the* Sliding down moonbeams *motif, which clearly established that gravity and fate were not the same thing.*

17. TERRIFIC TASKS

The girl has found her way to the enchanted son of the witch, whom she loves. The witch won't let them marry unless she can perform three terrific tasks. If she can't perform them, the witch will turn her to stone. The next morning, the girl wakes to find the forest around her ablaze. The witch shrieks that she must put out the fire. She can't and the fire is spreading rapidly. Summoning the witch's son by the power of love, she tells him what must be done and he uses the magic he has learned from the witch to call up storm clouds, which burst in a deluge that soon douses the flames. The witch's son disappears.

Next, she must build the witch a castle in a day using a pile of rocks. The witch's son, again summoned by love, hurls all the rocks into the air. When they come down, they rapidly form into a marvellous castle. The witch's son disappears again.

Lastly, the witch sets the task of finding a ring of power and knowledge that sank in a vast lake nearby. The witch's son, summoned by love, appears again and becomes a fish, dives down and soon emerges with the ring. At once he is in human form again, but this time he does not disappear - the girl's love has half broken the enchantment on him. The witch, hissing her annoyance, demands the ring, but the witch's son tells the girl to slip that ring onto her own finger. She does so and instantly has the knowledge and power to command the witch to vanish .The witch is never seen again. The girl and the witch's son (now completely released from enchantment) use the ring to marry and rule the wonderful castle. If they're not dead yet, they're living there to this day.

The terrific tasks (or tasks of difficulty) is a motif that can be found in many wonder tales across the world. The game below is set out for 3 players/teams **A, B & C**.

First a story containing the terrific tasks motif is told to or read by all. Use the *Imaginer* described in Part 3 of this book to get to know it thoroughly in imagination. **A, B & C** are given their roles (in the example, **A** = girl; **B** = witch; **C** = witch's son).

Now

- Players **A** explain who they are and describe themselves, their motives etc. (e.g to rescue a parent/child/lover etc). They are not the girl (as in the example here) but could still be another kind of (young or old) female in a different time, or (equally) a man or an animal or whatever else. **A** must not describe **C** beyond saying what he/she is (parent, child etc).

- Players **B** explain who they are, choosing a character like the model (witch = sorcerer/mad genius etc.) that will work well with what **A** has already explained. Again **C** must not be described in detail.

- Players **C** follow suit but must take into account what both **A** and

B have already explained, qualifying and expanding this in as many ways as possible.

• **A** begins the story, explaining how she/he has a power equivalent to the power of love in the example – or perhaps the same power, expressed differently, for example in playing a musical instrument with passion.

• **B** explains what the first task will be - not the same as in the model but equally fantastic and 'impossible'.

• **A** tells of how she/he summons **C** (This might be varied with each task.)

• **C** explains how, when summoned, she/he performs this task.

• The last three stages described above are repeated for tasks 2 and 3.

• When all tasks are complete, **A & B** describe how they get rid of or escape from the wicked task setter.

• Another 2 rounds can be played, changing roles each time.

Finally: (optional) The story details emerging so far in any round are noted and later retold in more developed form. In a group situation, players might also use this new story in a 'tale stretching' game from Book 3 *Yarn Spinning*.

General: This is quite elaborate, so with children it can be played initially with the whole groups divided into 3 and with the workshop leader coaching each group, getting as many suggestions as possible before choosing one for each stage. Details not matching the model or differing too much can be challenged by other groups. Something like the procedure in this game can be adapted to suit other story plots with a limited number of protagonists (any more than 5 can be tedious). It can also be adapted as a group writing exercise.

Story skills: This game requires close listening, quick thinking and sure-

footed improvisation, essential skills for storytellers.

Interesting: *A central metaphor in this tale is the liberation of the 'loved one' through a very personal quality sincerely exercised, in turn a liberating notion for many people, especially when the imagination becomes more involved. This is what the game can do when played in more 'serious' contexts.*

18. THE MAGIC OBSTACLES.

The Prince wants to marry the Rakshasha king's daughter and has passed three terrific tasks set for him with her help. Now the demon king, apparently agreeing to the wedding, sends him to invite his brother to the celebrations. The daughter gives him a box of stones, a flask of water and a tinder box with instructions to cast them behind him if ever pursued. When he arrives at the brother's palace, riding his horse, this huge Rakshaha understands the treacherous message and chases the prince to kill and eat him. When he's about to be caught, the prince throws down the box of stones, which becomes a mountain range. That stops the Raskshasha in his tracks whilst the prince gallops on – but not for long, because the Rakshasha climbs over the mountains and races on at great speed. When he's again about to be caught, the prince throws down the water from the flask, which becomes a sea and once more the Rakshasha halts whilst the prince hurtles on. But still he's not safe, because the Rakshasha swims over the sea and sprints at lightning speed towards him. The prince throws down the tinder box and a gulf of fire separates him from the doomed Rakshasha. He gets back safely, is married to the princess and makes his escape from the Rakshasha court with her.

Like *The Magic Chase* (No 10) and *Terrific Tasks* (No 16), the magic obstacles is a motif that migrates from one fairy/wonder tale and myth to another. This version is loosely summarised from a tale in *The Ocean of Story*, Somadeva's 10th Century Indian classic. The game based on it is a more complicated form of magic chase and again is for 2 players or teams (**A** & **B**). In this description, **A** is the escaper (prince) and **B** is the wicked chaser (Rakshasha). **A** aims to escape, **B** to catch.

First

• **A** chooses and writes down secretly on separate slips of paper 3 'protections' (as given by the princess in the example story). These are based (roughly) on 3 out of the 4 elements (earth – air – fire -water), for example a bag of soil or rocks, a small windmill, a box of matches or a bottle of lemonade.

• Meanwhile **B** (also secretly) writes on a single slip which of the 4 elements he/she can be beaten by (e.g. *fire will burn me, but water and earth and air I can find ways to move over and through*). Both slips are placed face down between players. This can be repeated immediately with players roles reversed, so that the next round can continue straight away.

Now

• Players **A** describe how they are escaping from the wicked chaser (e.g. on horseback, in a car, astride a dragon etc.). In the process, **A** can (when the game is familiar) send out small 'testers' containing the lethal elements - dragon's fiery breath, drops of sweat etc.

• **B** describes how they will catch up (running very fast, flying, swimming) and how the.testers will be avoided. This can give **A** clues as to which element is the weakness, so a clever answer may include false clues (e.g. the chaser might be wearing flame/water/windproof armour even though rocks (earth) would kill him/her).

• **A** chooses which thing/element to throw down and how it will be transformed into an obstacle to stop the wicked one. If this element in the thing is the 'killer', **B** must say so and the round stops there. If not, players **B** say how they will get over the magic obstacle and go on chasing.

• **A** puts down the second obstacle and says how it transforms.. Again, if this obstacle is based on the element that is the 'killer', the game ends there. If not, chasers (**B**) must explain how they get past that obstacle and go on chasing.

• **A** puts down the third and final obstacle. If it's based on the killer element, the wicked chaser (**B**) is beaten. If not, the escaper is caught (**A** loses). But for the round, **B** scores 1 point if killed by the first obstacle, 2 if killed by second, 3 if it's the 3rd , but 6 if he/she catches the escaper.

• The next round is played with **A** as the wicked chaser and **B** as the escaper. Points scored by **A** and **B** as chasers in the two rounds determine who wins this pair of rounds..

Finally: Each round has made a different version of this motif/plot for telling or writing.

General note: Because of the extra complication, it's better to play this game when games like The Magic Chase have first been mastered, maybe leaving out the 'testers' notion until it's well established. The 'elements' idea needs to be thoroughly explored with children, so that they see what transformations should be possible. If the final re-telling stage is to be included, it's useful to record details immediately after each round in some way – game details can be too easily forgotten.

Story Skills: The excitement of this game can provoke players. into the imaginative leaps involved in good story making. The ability to transform any motif like this one and also to explore this particular kind of 'elemental transformation' whilst following the 'rules' is very much a storyteller's skill. Clues and bluffs develop descriptive abilities, written and spoken.

Interesting: This game can have a useful edge in more sensitive work with individual children if, keeping up the playful feel, there is just faintest hint of a correspondence between chaser and whatever person/thing/situation etc is (say) feared (or whatever) by the child. In this case, it's the job of the counsellor, teacher etc. to make sure the child does get away and the chaser is destroyed, by subtle cheating or by coaxing them through the stages.

19. THE BIRD OF TRUTH

Three brothers who have wandered as penniless beggars with no idea of their origins set off in turn to climb the blue Mountain of Truth. At the top of it is a white bird and in front of that bird are 2 piles of dust, one white and one blue. If you can climb to the top of the mountain, looking the bird in the eye and ignoring all distractions, the bird will fly into the air taking some of the white dust, which it will sprinkle over you and you will have the truth. If you turn away, the dust is from the blue pile and you are turned to a blue stone on the mountainside. From this fate you can only be rescued by someone with the power that comes from looking the bird in the eye. It is very difficult to do this not only because the bird seems bigger, fiercer and more daunting the closer you climb to it, but also all the rocks on the hillside call out and create tempting visions and other distractions.

The first brother climbs up some of the way, but the many marvellous distractions on the mountainside eventually make him look away and he is turned to stone. The second gets further but suffers the same fate when the first one calls to him for help. The third gets all the way up, looks the bird in the eye and receives the white dust. This he does by blocking his ears with wax and cotton wool before he begins the climb. With the power of truth, he rescues his 2 brothers and many of the other captives on the mountainside. He also discovers that the 3 of them are princes, cheated of their inheritance by a wicked uncle. With the help of the grateful people rescued from the mountain, he and his brothers win back the kingdom. As to whether they live happily afterwards, that's another story.

This plot is contained within many other longer fairy/wonder tales, for example *Farizad of the Roses Smile* from *The Arabian Nights* or *The*

Fine Greenbird from Italo Calvino's *Italian Folktales*. Interestingly for those involved with gender issues, in the Arabian Nights version, the third one is the sister of the two brothers who fail.

The game is for a group

First: Together invent an alternative scenario - a walk through a dark forest or across a desert or down a long, lonely street. Change the bird to another creature and (perhaps) have it represent something else – knowledge, power, strength etc.

Now

• Three 'climbers' are chosen and leave the room. They must think up a strong reason for 'getting the bird' – why they want desperately to get its power. They must each write down 2 things that would 'ring all their bells' and be certain to distract their characters (*a million pounds in cash, a beautiful lady, a poisonous snake etc.*). Also a third thing, different for each of them, that would distract only their character. This list must be kept secret and given into the care of a referee (workshop leader etc). Other character details can be discussed and thought through in any remaining time.

• Meanwhile, the other players discuss possible distractions – things they guess 'climbers' will have written down. Players decide who will present particular distractions – money-based, fame-based, fear- based etc. Each person must prepare a mini-story about his or her distraction – not just '*there is money*' but '*Suddenly an enormous case opens in front of you and you see stack after stack on golden coins and wad after wad of notes etc*).

• The first 'climber' comes in and describes his/her motivations for 'climbing' (etc.) and answers up to 5 questions from the group about character type, history etc. The group can try to glean clues about the character and what will distract him/her.

• 'Climbers' pick any player/group to offer a distraction. As long as this doesn't match or resemble something on the list of 'bells', 'climbers' describe how they will get past it. If it does, they are turned to stone at that distraction and sit down beside the player/group offering that distraction. (Referees check and make decisions on resemblance.)

• If the 'climber' can get past a pre-agreed number of different distractions (say 7) without having any bells rung, he/she wins through. In the (optional) point scoring version, he/she would then get the maximum points (e.g.7), whilst if falling by the wayside, there would be points for the number of distractions passed previously. (1 to 6) The total score would be the aggregate of all three 'climbers'.

• The 2 other climbers follow in turn and go through the same procedure. Note that, if the previous climber has failed, he/she will be sitting beside a possibly dangerous distraction that might be avoided – though he/she might have been caught by the single personal 'bell', so climbers can take a chance..

Further rounds can be played with different scenarios and climbers. (In a point scoring game, rounds would be compared to find the winners.)

General note: *This calls for some role playing – the 'climbers' have to describe who they are and answer questions about themselves (their characters). Distracters can also be encouraged to do their distracting in role– like sharp sales people talking up a product or barrow boys in a market. The game needs to be adjusted to suit age and experience. It works best when the original story is first densely imagined. A good way to do this is to use the Imaginer from Part 3 of this booklet, game nos. 21 & 22..*

Story skills: *Often thought of as an acting skill, role playing is very much part of narrative ability. Shrewd observation and guesswork is called for on both sides, whilst descriptive skills are stretched in creating the distractions. A round of the present game, incidentally, leaves a good structure for a group narration, each climber telling his/her part in the tale, each distracter chiming in at the right moment and perhaps a central narrator giving the overall shape to the plot.*

Interesting: This game can be adjusted as an exercise in empathy and sensitivity for groups of people getting to know each other better and/or facing challenges such as addiction, behaviour problems etc. 'Climbers' will not be in role and will be encouraged to write down things that really will 'ring their bells' – loudly. Distractions are based on what the rest of the group know or suspect will be 'bells'. Climbers have the option of explaining how they will get past any distraction, even if it does ring bells. Whilst playing games around serious concerns can seem frivolous, it can have some very strong effects.

20. SPELLBOUND CASTLES AND STONE STATUES

A ruined castle stands alone and ruined, under a dreadful spell. The gardens all around are filled with briars and brambles; the fountains are silted up. Inside the broken walls are stone statues. These are the people who once lived there, transformed by the power of magic to stand literally petrified for all of time, unless someone should come to release them and to bring the castle also back to life. But to do that, they will have to brave dangers and trials...

The traditional image of the enchanted castle (or similar place) crops up widely in ancient oral and literary traditions as well as in more modern fantasy - younger players may know the classic witch's castle in *The Lion, the Witch and the Wardrobe* by C.S.Lewis, at least from the popular film version. The castle is sometimes paired with the stone statues (or similar figures) that can be revived,

This game can develop either or both of these symbols (or similar images. ('Similar images' can include 21st Century settings not involving obvious magic - deserted warehouses, disused stations etc.) It is yet another partner or group game and also works well as a solo imagining and plotting exercise. As described here, it's an advanced game for quite skilled players

First do some imagining around the idea of an enchanted castle or stone statues or any similar images, agreeing on the image first. You can use the *Imaginer* described in the next section to do this more systematically. Afterwards swap ideas and 'visions' with a partner or a group (or review these if playing solo). Agree on general description and features of the castle.

Then (in a pair or group game) decide who will be **A** and who will be **B** and spend some time separately working out some basics, so that before starting the game below,

> • **A** will know (and keep secret) how the enchantment works and what weaknesses it has (it must have weaknesses).
> • **B** will work out a profile of the hero or heroine (or both) who will break the spell, based on the what **A** and **B** have already agreed about the castle. Characters and their skills/powers can be developed further during the game.

Now: *(For the purposes of explanation, we'll use the enchanted castle in what follows. It should be possible to adapt other images of this kind, given a little ingenuity and some practice in transposing plot ideas.)*

> • **A** spins the wicked plot, elaborating how and why the castle is enchanted, when it happened, how the power works, what is dangerous for anyone going there. Three clues about the limits and weaknesses in the power and how it can be defeated should be cleverly slipped into this, but not directly stated. (For example, *'The cold and the damp is kept constant and no light is allowed to enter...'* suggests the possibility that light and warmth might have something to do with breaking the spell – which already gives 2 of the 3 clues).

> • **B** asks **A** up to (say) 7 questions about this to get a clear idea of the castle and how the magic might be working. He/she is not allowed to ask directly for the secret of any limits and weakness,

but can ask questions that might confirm suspicions. (*What kinds of things might happen if a candle were lit somewhere in that place?*) **A** must answer but can do so confusingly (*Blood could stir and pulses quicken and then a hiss and silence..*: - suggesting that it could begin to break the spell but might not do so completely).

• **B** now has to do some storytelling, describing the hero/heroine and how she or he goes to the castle – camouflaged perhaps or by a secret passageway or on a flying carpet. Anything is possible as long as it is a) explained as part of the storytelling and b) does not give the hero or heroine supreme powers. (For example, a cloak of invisibility is possible, but not a suit or armour that protects against all magic and makes the wearer strongest in all the world.)

• **A** challenges any part of the storytelling that doesn't square with what has already been said about the enchantment. *(If he flies into the castle on a magic carpet, he'll get caught in the huge magic spider's webs I said covered the whole place.... If the moonlight touches her, remember she'll be turned to stone.)* **B** must adjust the storytelling to cope with these challenges.

• Once in the castle, **B** describes how the hero or heroine makes the first attempt to break the spell. If this is way off the mark, **A** says 'cold'. If it's near but not quite there, **A** says 'warm'. **A** can also make challenges about the logic here (*'You said she lit a big fire, but with what in a cold, damp place like that?'*). Again **B** must explain (*'The magic carpet fetches dry wood and tinder instantly on command'.*).

• **B** can ask **A** for some storytelling about the castle and the history of its enchantment after cold or warm guesses. **A** should again drop at least 2 more hints about breaking the spell into this, but can hide these amid false leads etc

• The storytelling – guessing – storytelling etc. goes on until **B** guesses correctly or gives up. **A** should, however, give broader hints each time, trying to lead **B** to the answer.

Then (optional) **A** & **B** improvise in alternation at least 10 things (5 each) that will happen when the spell breaks (**A** *The whole castle is suddenly lit up in bright sunlight and birds are singing in the gardens...* **B** *The stone statues slowly begin to pulse with life and gradually to move...*

Finally turn the sequence in the game into a tale to tell. Tell it.

General note: This elaborate motif-based game draws on many of the skills developed through the series and can be a lot of fun to play for suitably skilled players. With older children, it works best if the workshop leader or teacher takes part A and gets the group as B to tell tales of the hero/heroine and the breaking of the spell (or whatever). He/she can then drop very broad hints, perhaps role playing a wizard or witch or other enchanter. As pointed out, the fairy tale setting in the example can be altered to quite different modern or futuristic or fantasy settings.

Story skills: Imagining a plot through, making spontaneous inventions, questioning and adjusting, being stumped for a while and then finding new ideas, setting up clues and reading them in what one has invented already – these are all part of the practical experience of story makers modelled in this game. Compare the optional final listing of effects with No.16 Magic Bags *in Book 3* Yarn Spinning.

Interesting: The language of fairy tale and myth contains some extraordinary and wonderful 'psychological maps' in symbolic form. The enchanted castle and its liberation is one such resonant image and can be very helpful in work with all kinds of psychological and psychosomatic conditions. The game is one way of involving clients and students in the imaginative optimism of it.

PART 3.
THE IMAGINER: SOLO GAMES

This section features a special imagining device you can make for yourself – in your imagination of course. The games in it work alongside any of the other games in this book and elsewhere in the series. They are ways of making old stories new and of making new stories from old ones 'inside the head' at any suitable time and place. Stories are perhaps the most portable and invisible art form, so this could be anywhere safe enough to concentrate inwardly at any time when there's enough space and peace. Like any other skill, imagining well comes with practice. The *Imaginer* is about practising the art of imagination.

MAKING THE IMAGINER

First: Spend some time carefully imagining and building in your mind's eye this special imagining structure. It is for playing through and reviewing stories and is a very personal thing, so there's no set form. Some people like to adapt everyday technology, like TVs or DVD players with remote functions. Others prefer more 'storyish' things like crystal balls, magic mirrors, strange boxes and bags, castles or palaces with many rooms and so on.

Some bits of this 'device' will work better than others to begin with. If you are good at mental pictures, the picturing part may work much better than the smell bit. If you're good at feelings, this may be stronger than sound and so on. Given time, more or less all of it will work.

IMAGINER MODES & FUNCTIONS:

- It has a **zoom in** function – so you can look at the detail
- It has a **zoom out** so you can look at the whole pattern
- It has a **just picturing** so you can get just a picture or two alone
- There's a **just sounds** bit so you can concentrate on sounds

- Then there's **just feelings** – so you can concentrate on the mood and the way it makes you feel.
- There are also **just touch, just taste** and **just smells**. You might not need these at all stages of a story, but it's fun to play with them.
- There is a **blender** so you can mix up 2 or 3 or all of these, though this can take a while to master completely.
- Last but very importantly, there will be a **viewer** - a way you can look at 2 or 3 or even 4 different stories and scenarios (separate screens/globes, different rooms with open doors etc).

21. IMAGINE IT (THE IMAGINER 1)

Use the *Imaginer* to imagine a story you want to get absorbed in more thoroughly. It can be a very relaxing exercise to do this with with eyes closed, ideally sitting or lying in a reasonably comfortable position – though I've used this and other solo exercises when forced to stand up on crowded train journeys or when obliged to endure a boring speaker.

First: It's helpful to reduce the story to an outline frame, a set of episodes and essential points etc (see Part 1 of this booklet). Some like to write this down.

Now: Use the frame (written or remembered) to guide you through imagining each stage of the story, taking your time to 'look into the background' using the different modes of the imaginer – to notice some of the details you might not have noticed before. (For example, are there some things about the characters' looks or clothes or the sound of their voices or the feeling they give you that can come through more vividly?) Linger over each stage.

Finally: Tell the story over again but pause to 'consult' the imaginer for a few extra details every so often. Or take the story to a questioning game with others such as *Embroidery* (*Yarn Spinning*, No 1.) and perhaps rely on the *Imaginer* to help you answer queries.

22. NEW SUITS (THE IMAGINER 2)

This builds on the last game. You already have a vivid imagining of a tale and are able to 'bring it up' in the *Imaginer*, using at least some of the different 'modes' of imagining (sight, sound, feelings etc). You also have an outline frame to guide you. Now you want to make a new, transposed version.

First: Put your imagining of the tale in one 'profile' or 'view' on your imaginer (for example on a separate multi-sensory screen, in a separate crystal ball, room etc). Alternate this with mentally looking across to a blank view, a separate space or different profile where the new tale will be formed (e.g. another connected screen or crystal ball). It doesn't matter if this is only a vague idea and feeling at this stage.

Now

For each stage of the story as already explored, imagine a new equivalent stage in the transposed tale, with new but comparable characters, places, things etc. For example, suppose the old tale had a poor beggar girl in a medieval town. You have decided to substitute a hungry stray cat in an urban jungle. You hold the two images beside each other on the separate 'viewers' and see which bits of the imaginer you can get to work best to explore the detail of the new version. Also how you can keep your girl and cat and towns similar underneath. Work through all stages of the story thoroughly enough to give each 'mode' of imagining at least a chance. If any stick and don't work, simply move on. You don't have to get it all at once. Some modes might not be relevant anyway.

Finally: Tell the new tale through to yourself in a relaxed way, allowing details to emerge, perhaps sometimes to change. Or again use it in a questioning story game. Or simply try it on a sympathetic friend.

23. TELLING GLIMPSES (THE IMAGINER 3)

You have a story and are thinking of telling it out aloud in a more formal situation – perhaps in front of a larger group or class or even a public audience. You can use the *Imaginer* to rehearse doing this well and naturally, allowing it to change as necessary to suit the occasion.

First get to know the story thoroughly (perhaps through the previous 2 games), so that it is just as if you are remembering something you witnessed.

Now

• Keeping the whole tale up in one 'profile', use another 'view' on the *Imaginer* to take a good look at the situation(s) in which you could be telling the tale.

• You can make all kinds of adjustments. For example, if you want more confidence, you can make the listeners tiny and yourself larger. Or you might decide to zoom in on one or two encouraging listeners, so that you can be talking just to them.

• You can also listen to and watch and sense yourself telling the story well, getting it over to all your listeners, being successful.

• You can (and should) imagine carefully going a little bit wrong and then re-balancing so that you can pick it up again – everyone makes mistakes, so it's worth practising making them 'invisible'.

• Sometimes you use the *Zoom Out* function to watch yourself from the outside for a while, as if you were a friendly audience member. Sometimes you can let the *Imaginer* take you right inside yourself telling the story well.

• You can alternate all these 'experiments' with just getting really absorbed in the 'landscape' of the story on the original 'view' in the *Imaginer*.

• If you like, you can even imagine cheers and applause at the end.

Finally: Just do it.

24. MAGIC PURSES AND GOLDEN GEESE
(THE IMAGINER 4.)

A good story is like one of those fairy tale magic purses that are never empty: there is always new value in it if you look. Or you could compare it to the golden goose: you can trust it to keep on delivering the golden eggs - as long as you don't kill the 'bird' by analysing it and fixing it in one form. This 'game' is a way of building up 'trust in the gold' in a tale (or group of tales) and of seeding the ground so that new ways of telling it and new versions can 'spring up' as and when necessary.

First: Choose a tale you already know quite well. You might even have taken it through all three of the other *Imaginer* games, but want to get a glimpse of more possibilities.

Now: Bring up a sense of the whole story in the *Imaginer* and try these starting points for brief imaginings. Use modes of the *Imaginer* to intensify them, then let them go and move on.

• Imagine the story as something abundant – a treasure vault, a fountain, a garden, a feast or whatever appeals.

• Think of an image of mystery veiling a part of the story. Imagine the feel of sharpness as that part of the story comes clearly.into focus.

• Take an important item from the story, for example the ring in

The Talisman (see No. 4 *Flesh on Bones* p.11). Imagine it in detail in more than one form. Recall and imagine similar things in other stories (e.g. rings of power, enchantment etc; rings in pigs' noses).

• Think of and imagine a random series of things this item could become in a new version of the tale – a tree, a stone, a piece of string etc. Imagine how this might change the rest of the tale. (No need to make full versions.)

• Do something similar with single happenings and motifs in the story (e.g.opening a door; walking along a road; losing something etc)

• Between brief imaginings, clear the 'screen' and return to blank views and/or a relaxed and confident image of the tale you know. Do this for some time as you finish the exercise.

Finally let if all sit. Trust the story.

General note on the 4 Imaginer games: The *Imaginer is an entertaining way of couching some imaginative mental disciplines of the storyteller. It's helpful to review the simple suggestions in Book 2* Imagine On, *pages 6 & 7 if presenting these exercises to a workshop group/class etc – where it's vital to pick a moment when it's possible to quieten the group mood down. With children, it may take a while to establish this kind of quiet 'going inside' as a habit. Experience shows that this is more than worthwhile, paying back eventually in enhanced attention and imaginative capacity. Note that the* Imaginer *allows for different 'modes' of imagining. When we imagine, we represent to ourselves using images from the 5 senses and integrative 'whole pattern' things like feelings, moods etc. People imagine in different ways and favour particular 'modes', the visual being the most common, often combined with 'feel'. Other modes may develop more slowly and are not always needed in creating strong images..*

Here are some additional tips on solo imagining:-

- *Allow imagination to work 'by itself' 'with just a little direction. If it doesn't and you get no images, move on. Forcing it too much is a bit like trying to go to sleep by willpower.*

- *Imagining sometimes changes unexpectedly. If one is relaxed about it, this can simply be interesting, something one observes. New, unexpected and surprising 'picturings' can be as useful as more intentional ones.*

- *Being distracted by stray thoughts and all sorts more whilst imagining is common. It takes a while to learn to ignore this and return attention to the imagining – for adults as much as children.*

Story skills: *The* Imaginer *ideas develop a story maker's and teller's skill of inner focus and concentration. The first 3* Imaginer *games have clear goals coinciding with enhanced story skill. – No 21* Imagine It *makes sure a story is deeply known imaginatively, rather than just as an idea and an outline. No 22* New Suits *practises precisely the kinds of transposing skills worked on in this book and makes them work imaginatively on a personal level. No 23* Telling Glimpses *is of course about developing the important skill of performing a story to people, adapting and making it new as you go. The fourth and final game, No 24* Magic Purses and Golden Geese *is intentionally not endgaining – it's an exercise in imaginative expectation whose results can be left to simmer, a much more important thing than it might appear for all imaginative artists , who often have dozens of ideas 'cooking' at any one time.*

Interesting: *Learning to focus and control one's imagination is a life skill with all sorts of applications in both professional and personal life. It's perhaps too frequently neglected as a real and teachable skill in modern education, which overvalues the development of 'intentional' and analytical thought and appears to assume that imagination is sufficiently covered by 'imaginative subjects'. The* Imaginer *games can be seen as exercises in direct development of imagination. They teach forms of mental control and flexibility sometimes associated with things like meditation or self-hypnosis, though without the negative associations those words would have for some people. In* *counselling/therapeutic/personal education contexts, there are clients/ students who can benefit from taking a long, lingering look at a story packed with resonant and suitable metaphors in this way whilst simultaneously learning to relax 'imagination muscles', accepting and integrating the random and irrational. The technique in No 23 is similar to techniques used in coaching all kinds of performance skills and can be used to rehearse other life skills effectively. Note that the kind of imagining and then letting go demanded by No 24* Magic Purses & Golden Geese *can teach some very helpful and subtle lessons about experience and memory.*

ABOUT THE AUTHOR

For well over two decades, Rob Parkinson has told his tales in all kinds of places, from theatres, festivals, schools and libraries to pubs and clubs and restaurants and zoos and even shacks in the Australian outback. A varied career path prior to becoming a professional storyteller included teaching, driving trucks and taxis, restoring antiques, playing guitar in bars, painting signs and travelling extensively – and provided vital experience to draw on as a tale teller. He has chaired the Society for Storytelling, run a story club and appeared in front of millions of television viewers reciting Chaucer's tales and playing some of his ancient instruments. His unique fantasy songs for children have continued to prove enormously popular across a broad age range.

In recent years, Rob has focused his attention on the uses of stories in education, therapy, counselling and communication in general. In addition to his work as as a tale teller, he has a successful practice as a Human Givens therapist and runs training courses for professionals in all walks of life. He has published numerous articles and papers on storytelling and is the author of Transforming Tales - How stories can change people.

Imaginary Journeys focuses on positive uses of imagination, very much including storytelling. Visit our website to view the full range we are developing or write/telephone for information.

www.imaginaryjourneys.co.uk
27 London Road, Tonbridge, Kent UK TN10 3AB UK
Tel/fax ± 44 (0)1732 362356
info@imaginaryjourneys.co.uk